TO BE
NOBODY
ELSE

by John Pearson

ACKNOWLEDGEMENTS
The author wishes to thank the following
sources for permission to quote from copy-
righted material used in this book:

HOUGHTON MIFFLIN CO.: The quotations from
Let Us Now Praise Famous Men by James Agee
are used by permission of the publishers,
Houghton Mifflin Co., copyright 1941 by
James Agee and Walker Evans.

HARCOURT, BRACE & WORLD, INC.: for permission
to quote from *Poems 1923-1954* by E. E. Cummings,
E. E. Cummings: A Miscellany Revised, and from
The Diary of Anais Nin, Volume Two 1934-1939,
copyright 1967 by Harcourt, Brace & World, Inc.

GEORGE EASTMAN HOUSE: for permission to quote
from *The Daybooks of Edward Weston,* Volume II,
published by George Eastman House and Horizon
Press.

The author also wishes to express appreciation
to Wayne Miller, Tom Baird, and Joe and Meri Ehrlich
for their help, criticism, and encouragement.

Designed by Tony Fry

Ballantine Books' Edition

First Printing: April, 1969

Printed in the United States of America.

BALLANTINE BOOKS, INC.
101 Fifth Avenue, New York, N.Y. 10003

To Liz

To be nobody-but-yourself in a world which is doing its best, night and day, to make you everybody else—means to fight the hardest battle which any human being can fight, and never stop fighting.

—e. e. cummings

Only as long as we can laugh
at ourselves are we nobody else.
—*e. e. cummings*

The only world I know without
walls, is that of illusion
and poetry. For me that is
the only liberation. I don't
believe man can be changed by
outer systems. It has to
come from within.
—from The Diary of Anais Nin

Which part of me is me?
—*a four year old*

The young child is looking in the world to find himself—
reflected in a mirror with a thousand faces.
—*Maria Montessori*

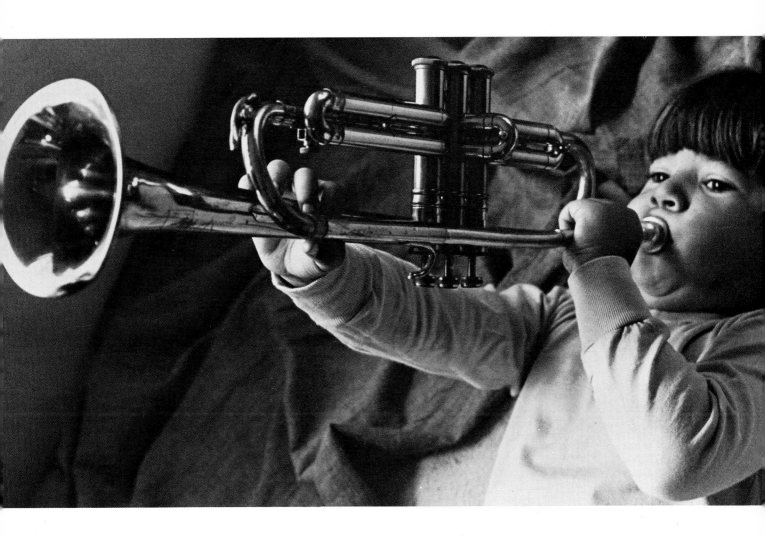

If God is just in your mind, how did he start everything?
—*a six year old*

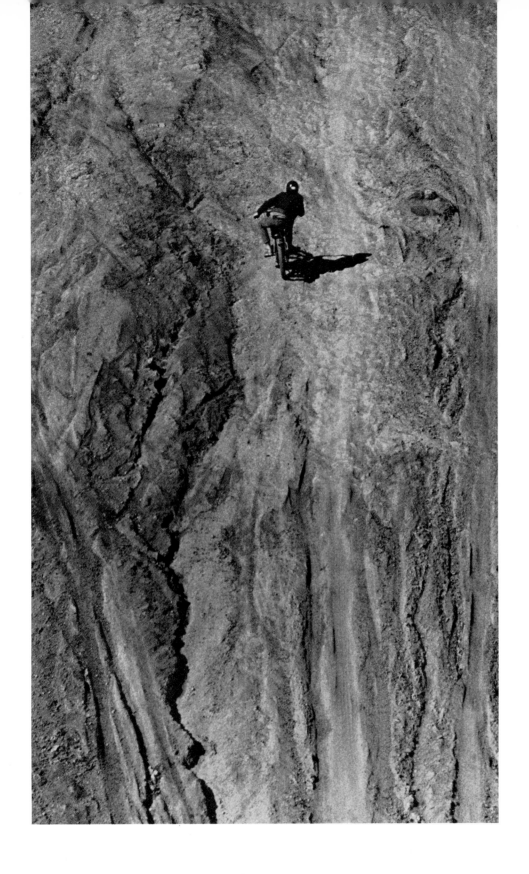

I exist as I am — that is enough.
—*Walt Whitman*

I am the adventurer on a voyage of discovery, ready to receive
fresh impressions, eager for fresh horizons...to identify myself in,
and unify with whatever I am able to recognize as significantly
part of me—the "me" of universal rhythms.
　　　　　　　—from The Daybooks of Edward Weston

i thank you God for most this amazing
day: for the leaping greenly spirits of trees
and a blue true dream of sky; and for everything
which is natural which is infinite which is yes.
                                        —e. e. *cummings*

...which is natural

...which is infinite

. . .which is yes.

...and this is the weaving of human living:
   of whose fabric each individual is a part:
   each is intimately connected with the
   bottom and the extremest reach of time:
   and not one of these things nor one of these persons
   is ever quite to be duplicated nor replaced:
   but each is a new and incommunicably tender life,
   wounded in every breath, sustaining, for a while,
   without defense, the enormous assaults of the universe.

—from Let Us Now Praise Famous Men
by James Agee and Walker Evans

. . . and this is the weaving of human living:

of whose fabric each individual is a part:

. . . each is intimately connected with the
bottom and the extremest reach of time:

...and not one of these things nor one of these persons is ever quite to be duplicated nor replaced:

...but each is a new and incommunicably tender life...

. . . wounded in every breath . . .

. . . sustaining, for a while, without defense . . .

the enormous assaults of the universe.
—*from Let Us Now Praise Famous Men
by James Agee and Walker Evans*

We can never be born enough. We are human beings;
for whom birth is a supremely welcome mystery, the
mystery of growing: the mystery that happens only
and whenever we are faithful to ourselves.

—*e. e. cummings*

...the mystery that happens...

. . . whenever we are faithful to ourselves.

—*e. e. cummings*